THE BLACKWELL GUIDE TO CD RECORDING

VOLUME ONE

The recordings experts at Blackwell review
their personal choices of the classical "must have"
CDs for anyone wishing to build their own library

THE BLACKWELL GUIDE TO CLASSICAL RECORDINGS

VOLUME ONE

WRITTEN BY
Katherine Cooper, Sally Outen, Luke Wilcox, Ben Hall, Tom West, Rachel Parris, Luke Berryman, Hugh Brunt

PUBLISHED BY
B. H. Blackwell, Beaver House,
Hythe Bridge Street, Oxford, OX1 2ET
www.blackwell.co.uk

DESIGN BY
The One Off
www.theoneoff.com

PRINTED & BOUND BY
Joshua Horgan
246 Marston Road, Oxford, OX3 0EL
www.joshuahorgan.co.uk

FIRST PUBLISHED
2007

FOREWORD

Jeremy Summerly is the conductor and founder of the Oxford Camerata, a choir specialising in early music. As well as his conducting commitments, he is a lecturer at the Royal Academy of Music, and has written and presented for BBC Radio 3. The combined work of Jeremy Summerly and the Oxford Camerata has produced numerous excellent recordings, but of particular note is the recording of Tallis' *Spem in Alium* which was at the top of the Blackwell classical CD chart almost consistently for its first fifteen months of release.

> " I arrived as an undergraduate in Oxford in the year of the Blackwell centenary. In those days Blackwell Music Shop was in Holywell Street, and it nestled neatly between the Holywell Music Room and the King's Arms. As a music student at New College there were few incentives for me to venture beyond this quaint street. This should have been because the University Music Faculty was itself located in the Holywell, but my memory is that - however shamefully - the allure of Blackwell and the King's Arms was that much greater. After three years of study, my Blackwell account revealed that I had spent exactly one-third of my entire outgoings in their Music Shop (sensibly the King's Arms did not allow me credit). This was seen as extravagant by some, although a quarter of a century later that early collection of books, scores, and records forms the foundation of a substantial library that I would hate to be without.
>
> Although I am a professional musician, I recognise that I am also a boffin. I love music and I get excited about the way that it sounds and the way that people write about it.

This little book is the work of boffins, and it is a mine of enthusiastic and opinionated information compiled by people whose hobby, as well as their job, is music.

When I was a student, the commercial medium of music was the vinyl record rather than the compact disc. Consequently I have a large collection of LPs, many of which I still listen to today. Some of these LPs have been re-mastered, but by no means all of them. Fortunately, my very favourite recording of all time has been transferred onto CD, moreover at budget price, and I mention it here because it is my pick of the recordings reviewed in this guide. It's the RCA 1966 studio recording of Sir William Walton's First Symphony played by the London Symphony Orchestra under André Previn. Previn conducted (and continues to do so) this piece so well that BBC 2 once made an entire television programme about his performance of it alongside footage of Sir William himself. It strikes me that Walton is too often underrated - his First Symphony is a masterpiece by any standards. And yes, Sir William studied at Oxford University. I imagine he also shopped at Blackwell. ,,

Jeremy Summerly
East Oxford, August 2006

INTRODUCTION

The first Blackwell bookshop opened in Oxford in 1846 and has since grown into a national specialist bookselling chain, focusing primarily on academic titles.

Blackwell Music Shop first opened in Oxford in 1955 on Holywell Street, serving the academic community of Oxford University's Faculty of Music. The reputation of the Music Shop became synonymous with expertise and thanks to the superb in-depth knowledge of its staff and the high standard of customer service, it became the first choice of destination for many musicians. In 1999 the shop moved location to Broad Street, which is the heart of the Blackwell brand, opposite its famous flagship store and adjacent to the Blackwell Art & Poster Shop.

The Blackwell Music story continued with the acquisition of the Heffers brand in Cambridge in 1999. In many ways, the history of Heffers in Cambridge mirrors that of Blackwell in Oxford. Like Blackwell, Heffers was founded in the nineteenth century and has subsequently earned its place as a University institution.

The music department of Heffers was originally sited in the main Heffers shop, but in 1990 moved to its present location in a separate shop next door. The rich choral heritage of the colleges is of course a speciality of the shop, and many past members of the great college choirs have seen service in Heffers Sound.

Like Blackwell, Heffers staff pride themselves on exceptional knowledge, and are proud to be involved in the writing of this new CD Guide. As managers of the Blackwell Music Shop in Oxford and Heffers Sound in Cambridge, we are immensely proud of the collective knowledge held in our teams of staff, and we are certain that a vast number of our customers value that service as well.

Many of our customers ask our staff questions such as, "Which recording do you think is the best?" "How do you rate this recording?" "How good do you think the performers are on this disc?", and the opinions of the staff are trusted and valued. It was the idea of the team of Recordings staff themselves to write their own mini CD guides in which they would recommend and review their favoured recordings. The Recordings Specialist and her team fleshed out the idea into a package of guides, of which this is the initial introduction to "building a library".

We have produced a collection of 60 absolute must have works for anyone wanting a library of classical recordings, and the staff were challenged to select the best recordings of those 60 works, all of which are at budget- and mid-price. This first mini CD guide therefore provides an ideal collection of superb recordings for anyone wanting to start their own CD library. Subsequent guides will focus on full price recordings for specific genres of music such as Opera, Early Music, Historical Recordings, and DVDs – look out for these in the future!

We hope you will enjoy these recommendations and we look forward to serving you again in the future.

Vanessa Williams
Manager, Blackwell Music, Oxford

Tony McGeorge
Manager, Heffers Sound, Cambridge

CONTENTS

COLLECTION ONE
TOP TEN CLASSICAL RECORDINGS WE LOVE

Bach, J. S. – Brandenburg Concertos (1708–1721)	12
Handel – Messiah (1742 revised 1751)	12
Mozart – Clarinet Concerto (1791)	13
Beethoven – Sonata for Piano No. 14 Moonlight (1801)	13
Wagner – Overtures (1843–1874)	14
Grieg – Piano Concerto (1868)	14
Bizet – Carmen Highlights (1875)	15
Tchaikovsky – Symphonies Nos. 4–6 (1877-1878, 1888 and 1893)	15
Rachmaninov – Piano Concerto No. 2 (1900–1901)	16
Gershwin – Rhapsody in Blue (1924)	16

COLLECTION TWO
TO EXPAND YOUR HORIZONS

Bach, J. S. – St John Passion (1724 revised c.1730 and again late 1740s)	18
Vivaldi – Concerti for Violin and Strings Four Seasons (1725)	18
Handel – Music for Royal Fireworks and Water Music (1749 and 1715–1717 revised 1736)	19
Mozart – Magic Flute Highlights (1791)	19
Haydn – Symphonies Nos. 99–104 (1793–1795)	20
Beethoven – Symphonies Nos. 5 and 6 (1807 and 1808)	20
Schubert – Symphonies Nos. 5, 8 and 9 (1816, 1822 and 1825–1828)	21
Berlioz – Symphonie Fantastique (1830)	21
Mendelssohn – Violin Concerto (1844)	22
Chopin – Piano Works (1829–1846)	22
Mussorgsky – A Night on the Bare Mountain (1867 re-orchestrated 1886)	23
Verdi – Aida (1871)	23
Tchaikovsky – Swan Lake Highlights (1876)	24
Saint-Saëns – Carnaval des Animaux (Carnival of the Animals) (1886)	24
Dvořák – Symphony No. 9 From the New World (1893)	25
Mahler – Symphony No. 5 (1901–1902)	25
Debussy – La Mer (1903–1905)	26
Stravinsky – The Firebird (1915)	26
Holst – The Planets (1916)	27
Shostakovich – Symphony No. 5 (1937)	27

COLLECTION THREE
IF YOU'RE FEELING A LITTLE MORE ADVENTUROUS

Tallis – Spem in Alium (c.1570)	30
Bach, J. S. – Organ Works (c.1700–1715)	30
Various – Baroque Suites and Concertos (1722–1749)	31
Mozart – Serenade No. 13 Eine kleine Nachtmusik (1787)	31
Haydn – String Quartets Opus 64 (1790)	32
Mozart – Requiem (1791)	32
Beethoven – Piano Concertos Nos. 2 and 5 Emperor (1793 revised 1794–1795 and 1809)	33
Schubert – Lieder (1815–1826)	33
Rossini – The Barber of Seville Highlights (1816)	34
Beethoven – Symphony No. 9 Choral (1822–1824)	34
Mendelssohn – Overtures (1824–1839)	35
Schumann – Symphony No. 1 Spring (1841)	35
Liszt – Piano Concertos Nos. 1–2 (1849 revised 1853/1856 and 1839 revised 1849–1861)	36
Smetana – Ma Vlast (1872–1879)	36
Bruckner – Symphony No. 4 (1874 revised 1878–1880 and 1886)	37
Tchaikovsky – Piano Concerto No. 1 (1875)	37
Brahms – Piano Concerto No. 2 (1878–1881)	38
Tchaikovsky – 1812 Overture (1880)	38
Sullivan (and Gilbert) – Yeomen of the Guard (1888)	39
Strauss, R. – Also sprach Zarathustra (1895–1896)	39
Elgar – Variations on an Original Theme Enigma (1898–1899)	40
Sibelius – Finlandia (1899 revised 1900)	40
Puccini – Opera Highlights (1893–1926)	41
Schoenberg – Five Orchestral Pieces (1909)	41
Vaughan Williams – The Lark Ascending (1914 revised 1920)	42
Walton – Symphony No. 1 (1931–1935)	42
Orff – Carmina Burana (1936)	43
Prokofiev – Romeo and Juliet Highlights (1938)	43
Messiaen – Turangalila Symphonie (1946–1948)	44
Adams – Shaker Loops (1983)	44

COLLECTION ONE

TOP TEN CLASSICAL RECORDINGS WE LOVE

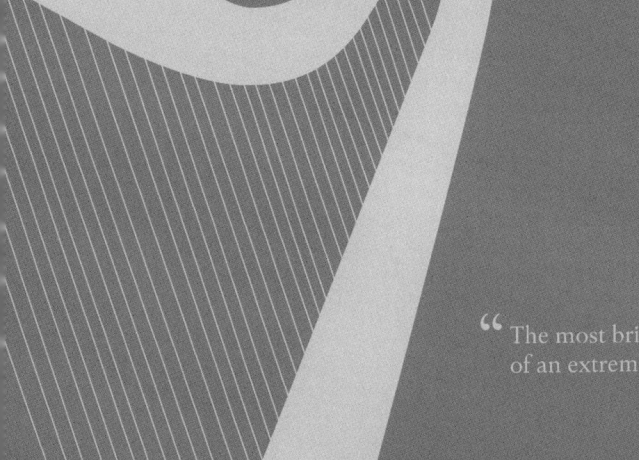

" The most brilliant and prolific member of an extremely musical family "

BACH, J. S. – BRANDENBURG CONCERTOS (1708–1721)
Neville Marriner, Academy of St-Martin-in-the-Fields
Philips 4709342 Released 3 June 2002

This 3 CD set is superbly good value; not only for the volume of music but for the quality of playing. This recording of a small group of performers on modern instruments is extremely well balanced with many moments of beautifully intuitive playing. Despite being recorded in the 1970s the sound quality is excellent and the acoustics have just the right amount of resonance to fill the sound, without swamping the clarity. The soloists include Jean-Pierre Rampal, Heinz Holliger, Maurice Hasson and Henryk Szeryng. As well as being an excellent recording this set also provides extremely detailed programme notes, covering from the history of the works commission and the alterations Bach made, plus some of the performance decisions Sir Neville Marriner has made. All round a very good recording - don't be put off by the ridiculously good price! Kath

If you like this, try J. S. Bach's *Orchestral Suites*

HANDEL – MESSIAH (1742 revised 1751)
Edward Higginbottom, Choir of New College Oxford
Naxos 857013132 Released 11 October 2006

This hugely popular 2006 recording of Handel's familiar masterpiece is conceived along the same lines as New College's equally successful *St John Passion* (also reviewed in this guide), and offers a truly refreshing interpretation of a work which has perhaps suffered from over-exposure. The home-grown soloists are well contrasted, delivering their arias with stylish ornamentation. Davies and Spence in particular are on glorious form, the latter sounding noticeably more like a baritone than usual whilst demonstrating remarkable vocal flexibility in 'Rejoice Greatly' (an aria traditionally allotted to the soprano). The three treble soloists are very well-suited to their respective arias, and the use of boys' voices in the tutti sections adds a buoyancy and clarity unmatched by many mixed-voice recordings. The Academy of Ancient Music play with their customary class and panache, underpinned by some sensitive and stylish continuo-playing. Kath

If you like this, try Haydn's *The Creation*

MOZART – CLARINET CONCERTO (1791)
Jack Brymer, Thomas Beecham, Royal Philharmonic Orchestra
EMI Classics 5675962 Released 3 September 2001

EMI have seen fit to re-release this disc as one of their 'Great Recordings of the Century', and rightly so. Jack Brymer is on fine form in the concerto, producing a convivial and perky sound for the jolly outer movements and a silky smooth and flowing legato for the all-important central Adagio. He is admirably supported by Sir Thomas Beecham and the Royal Philharmonic who come into their own in the exciting performance of the *Jupiter Symphony* which, along with a well-balanced rendering of the Bassoon Concerto played by Gwydion Brooke, completes this set. Tom

If you like this, try Mozart's *Flute and Harp Concerto*

BEETHOVEN – SONATA FOR PIANO NO. 14 MOONLIGHT (1801)
Vladimir Horowitz
RCA 82876623112 Released 8 November 2004

This sonata is so well known that it can be hard to bring off effectively. Horowitz manages to find something new in the incessantly beating triplets of the famous Adagio, painting a far more haunting picture than the usual all too serene moonlight imagery. The short Allegretto is witty and dance-like which adds to the shock of the final movement. Horowitz opts for a startlingly fast tempo which manages to serve not only the malevolence of the opening subject but also the lyricism of the brooding melody equally well. The sonata is coupled with fine accounts of the *"Appassionata"* and *"Waldstein"* sonatas. Recorded in 1956 and 1959 the disc has excellent sound for the time. Tom

If you like this, try Beethoven's Piano Sonata No. 8 *Pathétique*

WAGNER – OVERTURES AND BEST OF (1843–1874)
Various Artists
Naxos 8556657 Released 1 September 1997

Through the grandness of his vision, and in his attempts to achieve a perfect synthesis of poetry, theatre and music, Wagner totally transformed the face of opera. His work may seem a little inaccessible at first, but nobody should have any difficulties with this excellent selection of orchestral highlights from his operas. From the dreamy and romantic prelude to *Lohengrin*, to the stormily dramatic *Flying Dutchman* overture, this disc is a perfect reminder that there's so much more to Wagner than busty sopranos and horned helmets. Sally

If you like this, try Wagner's *Das Rheingold*

GRIEG – PIANO CONCERTO (1868)
Leif Ove Andsnes, Dmitri Kitayenko, Bergen Philharmonic Orchestra
Virgin Classics 5617452 Released 6 March 2000

The Norwegian pianist Leif Ove Andsnes has achieved legendary status for his interpretations of the music of his countryman Edvard Grieg (still not yet forty, he is already part of EMI's Great Performers of the Twentieth Century series) and this classy, understated take on the famous Piano Concerto makes it easy to see why. Displaying virtuoso vigour in the outer movements, Andsnes imbues the Adagio with a lyrical intimacy which anticipates his later success as a lieder pianist. The supremely popular concerto is nicely complemented by a masterly performance of the Piano Sonata and a handful of smaller-scale solo piano music including some of the charming Lyric Pieces. Kath

If you like this, try Grieg's *Holberg Suite*

BIZET – CARMEN HIGHLIGHTS (1875)
Placido Domingo, Georg Solti, London Philharmonic Orchestra
Decca 4582042 Released 16 February 1998

Few operas are as well known and widely loved as *Carmen*, and with good reason: its bright, vibrant score is full of memorable tunes (the 'Toreador Song' and 'Flower Song' come immediately to mind), and its tragedy and drama continue to touch audiences as they have for well over a century. This selection of highlights, energetically conducted by Solti, makes an excellent introduction to the opera; as Carmen, Troyanos is forceful and sultry, while Domingo makes a passionate Don Jose. Sally

If you like this, try Delibes' *Lakme*

TCHAIKOVSKY – SYMPHONIES Nos. 4–6 (1877, 1888 and 1893)
Evgeny Mravinsky, Leningrad Philharmonic Orchestra
DG 4775911 Released 13 March 2006

Tchaikovsky's gift for melody and colourful orchestration has established him as one of the world's favourite composers. His highly emotional music is full of his own internal struggles, relating to his sexuality and personal life - his Symphony No. 4 was written shortly after he fled an unhappy marriage, while the last movement of his sixth foreshadows his death. Under Mravinsky, the Leningrad Philharmonic Orchestra makes sympathetic and poignant renderings of these highly emotional works. Sally

If you like this, try Tchaikovsky's *Manfred Symphony*

RACHMANINOV – PIANO CONCERTO No. 2 (1900–1901)
Sviatoslav Richter, Stanislaw Wislocki, Warsaw Philharmonic Orchestra
DG 4474202 Released 1 May 1995

The Russian pianist Sviatoslav Richter was well-known for the vast range of his repertoire. He is best remembered, though, for his affinity with Russian music; his stunning interpretation of Rachmaninov's Piano Concerto No. 2 being just one reason why. Aside from the more immediately obvious highlights (Richter's deft dynamic control of those famous opening chords; his lyricism in the second movement; his virtuosity and clarity in the Finale, etc.), one is always conscious that Richter is considering the weighty work as a whole. His momentum gives a tremendous sense of direction to the work's dialogue, opening with despair and moving inexorably to the joyous Finale. An added bonus is the pairing with Tchaikovsky's Piano Concerto No. 1 (with Karajan conducting), which is an equally impressive performance. A recording not to be missed! Luke B

If you like this, try Rachmaninov's Piano Concerto No. 3

GERSHWIN – RHAPSODY IN BLUE (1924)
Leonard Bernstein, Los Angeles Philharmonic Orchestra
DG 4395282 Released 19 October 1993

This live CD, with Leonard Bernstein and the Los Angeles Philharmonic Orchestra, features three quintessential American works of the twentieth century. Think of the landscapes and soundscapes of this vast place and you may well imagine one of these pieces. In *Rhapsody in Blue*, Bernstein himself takes on the mighty piano part - a homage from one American maestro to another. This is Bernstein the jazz musician in full swing, with a certain cheek and musical swagger. Also featured are Barber's *Adagio for Strings* in all its poignancy and emotional intensity, and Copland's concert suite version of *Appalachian Spring*. At this price, you are guaranteed a treat. Ben

If you like this, try Gershwin's *An American in Paris*

COLLECTION TWO

TO EXPAND YOUR HORIZONS

"By character highly emotional and rather eccentric"

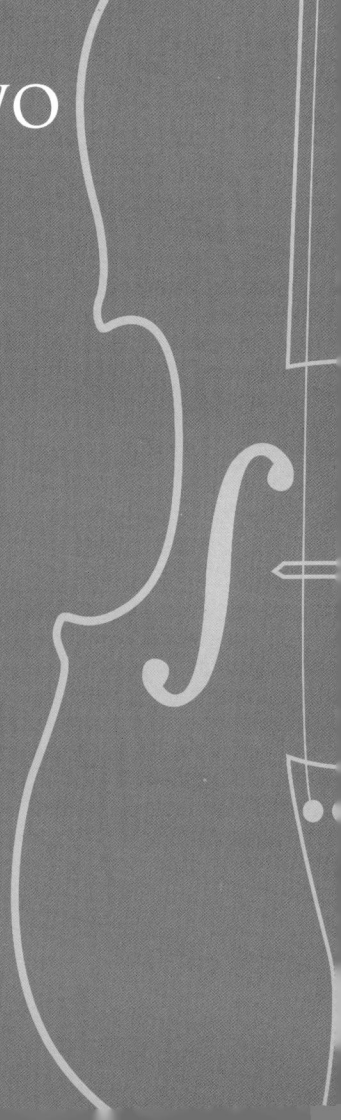

BACH, J. S. – ST JOHN PASSION
(1724 REVISED CIRCA 1730 AND AGAIN LATE 1740s)
Edward Higginbottom, Choir of New College Oxford
Naxos 855729697 Released 7 April 2003

This is the first recording of this landmark work to recreate the original conditions of performance. New College's *St John Passion* is performed on period instruments and uses male voices for the ripieni and for the arias, with three generations of New College singers taking the solo parts (James Gilchrist's fresh, involved Evangelist is a particular standout, narrating as if the familiar story of The Passion were being told for the first time). A sustained, dramatic, taut, and energetic rendering of Bach's masterpiece, this recording is remarkable for the clarity and intensity which the 'early-music' approach brings to the score. Kath

If you like this, try J. S. Bach's *St Matthew Passion*

VIVALDI – CONCERTI FOR VIOLIN AND STRINGS
FOUR SEASONS (1725)
Andrew Parrott, Taverner Players
Virgin Classics 4820882 Released 1 August 2005

This version of Vivaldi's masterpiece falls midway between the more restricted interpretation and thin texture (albeit authentic) of Hogwood and the Academy of Ancient Music, and the highly dramatic rendition by Nigel Kennedy and the English Chamber Orchestra. Generally, Parrott sets a fast pace, but keeps a tight rein, sometimes possibly too tight, such as in the Allegro of *L'Inverno*; John Holloway's violin, while beautifully intricate, is perhaps a little restrained, lacking some of the attack of Nigel Kennedy's powerfully fierce playing. The Presto of *L'Estate*, featuring Alison Bury, is invigorating, in contrast to the tense, emotive strains of *L'Autmno's* Adagio. By and large, the soloists perform excellently, and are well-supported by the full, rich tones of the Taverner Players. Rachel

If you like this, try Vivaldi's *L'Estro Armonico*

HANDEL – MUSIC FOR ROYAL FIREWORKS AND WATER MUSIC (1749 AND 1715–1717 REVISED 1736)
Orpheus Chamber Orchestra
DG 4767071 Released 14 February 2005

The Orpheus Chamber Orchestra play without a conductor, the players taking turns to listen and make suggestions about interpretation, which tends to result in clear textures and tight ensemble playing. These qualities are eminently suitable for two of Handel's most popular orchestral works. Mellow sounding modern instruments are coupled with fresh and brightly articulated playing which lends energy to the rippling faster movements. The Andante and Air from the *Water Music* are characterised by a delicate intimacy making them real highlights on this sparkling disc. Tom

If you like this, try Handel's Concerti Grossi

MOZART – THE MAGIC FLUTE HIGHLIGHTS (1791)
Bernard Haitink, Bavarian Radio Symphony Orchestra
EMI Classics 5747702 Released 6 August 2001

An ideal introduction to Mozart's stage works and to opera in general, this selection from Bernard Haitink's 1983 recording of *The Magic Flute* includes all of the major arias as well as generous selections from both finales. The cast are all native German speakers who successfully communicate the comedy and occasional pathos of the score: Siegfried Jerusalem's big-voiced, unusually heroic-sounding Tamino, and Edita Gruberova's glacial, sparkling Queen of the Night are particular highlights. Kath

If you like this, try Mozart's *The Marriage of Figaro*

HAYDN – SYMPHONIES Nos. 99–104 (1793–1795)
Thomas Beecham, Royal Philharmonic Orchestra
EMI Classics 5855132 Released 6 October 2003

Sir Thomas Beecham conducts the Royal Philharmonic Orchestra for the last six of Haydn's 104 symphonies. The pick of the bunch here has to be the energetic *"Clock"* Symphony (No. 101). The atmospheric introductory Adagio is followed by a thrilling Presto, a delicate Andante, a stirring Menuetto and a Finale full of flair. The *"London"* and *"Drum Roll"* Symphonies also receive very fine accounts, the Andante of the latter being just a touch on the slow side. These works are among Haydn's most popular and are a good answer to those who would describe him as 'a second rate Mozart'. Tom

If you like this, try Haydn's Symphony No. 94 *Surprise*

BEETHOVEN – SYMPHONIES Nos. 5 AND 6 (1807 AND 1808)
Roger Norrington, London Classical Players
Virgin Classics 5624892 Released 2 August 2004

One of Beethoven's greatest achievements was to totally revolutionize the form of the symphony. While his first two symphonies are in the classical mode, his third (the *"Eroica"*), was much more emotionally expressive and is often labelled as heralding the dawn of the Romantic era. From there, his symphonies increased in length and scale to culminate in the gargantuan ninth, the first to introduce a choral dimension. On this disc, Norrington and the London Classical Players are on fine form, giving lush, expressive performances of Beethoven's fifth and sixth symphonies, the former being famous for the distinctive "knocking of fate" motif that opens the first movement. Sally

If you like this, try Beethoven's Symphony No. 4

SCHUBERT – SYMPHONIES Nos. 5, 8 AND 9
(1816, 1822 AND 1825–1828)
Charles Mackerras, Orchestra of the Age of Enlightenment
Virgin Classics 5618062 Released 5 June 2000

This generous set presents three of Schubert's best-admired symphonies, including Brian Newbould's completion of the originally unfinished eighth symphony. These period-instrument interpretations are magnificent. The fifth is astonishingly crisp, and the small orchestral forces and rapid tempi place the emphasis on the work's classical elements. For the eighth, Mackerras musters a fuller, richer string sound, offset by clear, well-balanced winds, demonstrating Schubert's development towards a more 'Romantic' style. Newbould's completion sounds strange to ears accustomed to the eighth as a two-movement work. The completion is based on sound scholarship, however, and it is interesting to hear this work as Schubert may have intended it. Luke W

If you like this, try Schubert's Symphony No. 6

BERLIOZ – SYMPHONIE FANTASTIQUE (1830)
Colin Davis, London Symphony Orchestra
LSO Live LSO0007 Released 5 February 2001

By character highly emotional and rather eccentric, Berlioz might be considered the perfect model of a Romantic composer. His first symphony depicts a series of dreamlike scenes in which he encounters Harriet Smithson, a Shakespearean actress he developed an obsessive passion for. She is given a melodic motif (an "idee fixe") that reappears in each successive movement: at a ball, in a pastoral scene, in the march of her murderer (the artist himself) to the scaffold, and at a witches' sabbath, where she has been warped into a grotesque hag. This symphony seems to be somewhat of a favourite of Sir Colin Davis (he has recorded it four times), and his clear understanding of the music comes out in this, perhaps his most sensitive rendition of the piece to date. Sally

If you like this, try Berlioz's *Harold en Italie*

MENDELSSOHN – VIOLIN CONCERTO (1844)
Kyung-Wha Chung, Charles Dutoit, Montreal Symphony Orchestra
Decca 4609762 Released 13 September 1999

Kyung-Wha Chung made her debut performance with Mendelssohn's Violin Concerto at the age of nine, and she retains an affinity with and fondness for its music that is apparent in this sparkling, joyous account. This disc also includes her gloriously impulsive and passionate performance of Bruch's Violin Concerto, as well as that composer's lesser known *Scottish Fantasy,* a work that is by turns heartily carefree and hauntingly beautiful. Sally

If you like this, try Mendelssohn's Octet

CHOPIN – PIANO WORKS (1829–1846)
Dinu Lipatti
EMI Classics 5868262 Released 9 May 2005

Had he lived longer, Lipatti would doubtless have become a (perhaps 'the'!) pianistic giant of the twentieth century; as it is, we are left with a handful of magnificent recordings. As they are from the first half of the century the sound quality is not great, but Lipatti's playing easily compensates for this. The filigree writing in the virtuosic waltzes is thrown off with ease; equally impressive is his beautiful tone, which brings unparalleled lyricism to works such as the ninth waltz. These two aspects combine in the third Sonata in a truly magnificent rendition, giving a tantalizing insight into what could have been... Luke B

If you like this, try Chopin's Piano Concertos

MUSSORGSKY – A NIGHT ON THE BARE MOUNTAIN (1867 RE-ORCHESTRATED 1886)
Theodore Kuchar, Ukraine National Symphony Orchestra
Naxos 8555924 Released 3 March 2003

This excellent-value Mussorgsky disc offers the opportunity to compare the composer's original version of his famously demonic bacchanale *A Night on the Bare Mountain* with the more familiar orchestration by Rimsky-Korsakov: Mussorgsky's woodwind-heavy scoring is even more abrim with manic glee than its better-known counterpart. The disc also includes Ravel's brilliantly evocative orchestration of *Pictures at an Exhibition* (originally conceived by Mussorgsky as a solo piano piece) with the principals of the National Symphony Orchestra of Ukraine delivering characterful portraits of the frequently grotesque macabre subjects depicted. Luke W

If you like this, try Borodin's *Polovtsian Dances*

VERDI – AIDA (1871)
Jon Vickers, Georg Solti, Rome Opera Orchestra & Chorus
Decca 4607652 Released 18 January 1999

This is a superbly dramatic recording of Verdi's grandest opera. Jon Vickers as Radames combines power and sensitivity and is nobly heroic throughout. He even manages to sing the top B♭, which ends 'Celeste Aida', pianissimo as Verdi intended. Leontyne Price never loses her rich, shining tone, and sings her arias with control and beauty. Rita Gorr is a terrifying Amneris whose performance in the trial scene is worth the price of the disc alone. Solti conducts with great enthusiasm and the triumphal March and Ballet are brought off with great flair. However, it is the more introverted moments in the score which continue to live in the memory, and nowhere more than in the hushed finale 'O Terra Addio'. Tom

If you like this, try Verdi's *La Traviata*

TCHAIKOVSKY – SWAN LAKE HIGHLIGHTS (1876)
Herbert von Karajan, Vienna Philharmonic Orchestra
Decca 4663792 Released 13 September 1999

The *Swan Lake* is joined here with its sister suites the *Nutcracker* and *Sleeping Beauty* to produce a superior "highlights" style disc, the abridging having been done by Tchaikovsky himself. Herbert von Karajan and an elegant Vienna Philharmonic present glowing performances of all three pieces. The stirring finales here are confidently dramatic, the soaring melodies beautiful and moving. The playing is always alert and the strings particularly produce a full rich sound. Tom

If you like this, try Tchaikovsky's opera *Eugene Onegin*

SAINT-SAËNS – CARNAVAL DES ANIMAUX (CARNIVAL OF THE ANIMALS) (1886)
Charles Dutoit, London Sinfonietta
Decca 4307202 Released 11 September 1991

Saint-Saëns never intended this collection to be made public, written as they were for private performances by the cellist Lebouc. This recording shows why the work deserves public attention. Dutoit commands a fine ensemble, boasting Pascal Rogé and Christina Ortiz on the piano, and the deep romantic tones of cellist Christopher van Kampen. Highlights include van Kampen's stately 'L'Elephant', Rogé and Ortiz's delicate, impressionistic playing in 'Aquarium', and the family favourite, 'Le Cygne', superlatively performed, without the excess of schmaltz so often accorded to it. Dutoit achieves a playful, arresting rendition of Sains-Saëns' "private" work. Rachel

If you like this, try Saint-Saëns' *Danse Macabre*

DVOŘÁK – SYMPHONY No. 9 FROM THE NEW WORLD (1893)
Colin Davis, London Symphony Orchestra
LSO Live LSO0071 Released 8 August 2005

Famously used in the "Hovis" advertisements, the slow movement of Dvořák's *New World* Symphony, with its nostalgic cor anglais melody, remains one of the most enduringly popular classical themes. Throughout the symphony, Dvořák strived to capture the essence of Negro and Native American music, just as the Czech folk idiom resonates through his other symphonies. Davis brilliantly captures the lyricism of Dvořák's work, lending it a freshness and vitality that is rarely surpassed on record. Sally

If you like this, try Dvořák's earlier symphonies

MAHLER – SYMPHONY No. 5 (1901–1902)
Herbert von Karajan, Berlin Philharmonic Orchestra
DG 4474502 Released 12 February 1996

Arguably Mahler's most renowned work, his Symphony No. 5 stands as a total embodiment of death, love, tragedy and fear. Indeed, after its first performance in 1904, Mahler is reported to have said, "Nobody understood it. I wish I could conduct the first performance fifty years after my death". Just over one hundred years after its completion, it still remains one of the most demanding and challenging of scores for even the conductor and orchestra. This disc from the Berliner Philharmoniker, under Karajan, is well regarded as one of the finest recorded accounts of Mahler's masterpiece; exquisitely contrasting moments of utter emotional outpouring against the bleaker, dark passages of the symphony. Recorded in 1973 at the height of the orchestra's 'golden age' under Karajan, we are treated to a superb documentation of this canonic work on a remarkably satisfying mid-price disc. Hugh

If you like this, try Mahler's Symphony No. 1 *Titan*

DEBUSSY – LA MER (1903–1905)
Fruhbeck de Burgos, London Symphony Orchestra
Regis RRC1177 Released 5 April 2004

Subtle and impressionistic renderings of changing mood and tone, the works of Debussy are frequently compared to the paintings of Monet and Renoir. This disc includes three of Debussy's most well-known works: the orchestral seascape *La Mer*, the dreamy and sensuous *Prelude á l'apres midi d'un faune*, and the three poetic *Nocturnes*. Under the baton of Fruhbeck de Burgos, the LSO ably brings out the delicate detail of these pieces, while maintaining a refreshing sense of spontaneity throughout. Sally

If you like this, try Ravel's *Bolero*

STRAVINSKY – THE FIREBIRD (1910)
Kent Nagano, London Symphony Orchestra
Virgin Classics 4821062 Released 1 August 2005

Arguably the most innovative composer of the twentieth century, Stravinsky introduced the world to an entirely new range of sounds and rhythms. His music glows with bold orchestral colour, from the energetic, oriental-sounding *Firebird* Suite to *The Rite of Spring*, whose unrelentingly savage depiction of a virgin sacrifice plunges a knife into the sickening heart of Romanticism. Nagano and the LSO give spirited performances of these and other works, confidently riding the forceful dynamic of the music, and in particular, perfectly capturing the full spine-tingling intensity of *The Rite of Spring*. Sally

If you like this, try Stravinsky's *Petrushka*

HOLST – THE PLANETS (1916)
Simon Rattle, Philharmonia Orchestra
EMI Classics 5758682 Released 3 February 2003

From the harsh, stabbing chords of 'Mars', to the exhilarating main theme of 'Jupiter' (familiar from the anthem 'I vow to thee my country'), Holst's *The Planets* is arguably the most borrowed-from work of British classical music. Rattle's fresh interpretation brings out the full force of the orchestration, giving strongly contrasting characterisations of each of the seven movements. The suite is paired here with a studious and expressive interpretation of Britten's early masterpiece, the *Sinfonia da Requiem*. Sally

If you like this, try Britten's *Sea Interludes* from *Peter Grimes*

SHOSTAKOVICH – SYMPHONY No. 5 (1937)
Rudolf Barshai, West German Radio Symphony Orchestra
Regis RRC1075 Released 29 April 2002

Having fallen out of favour with the Soviet musical establishment due to the dissonant nature of his opera *Lady Macbeth of the Mtsensk District*, Shostakovich made his fifth symphony relatively conventional and accessible. The symphony was an immediate success on its premiere, and its air of forced rejoicing provides a fascinating insight into the mood in Russia during the time of the Stalinist purges. The work is paired here with the sixth symphony, in a clear and well-balanced performance conducted by seasoned Shostakovich interpreter Rudolf Barshai. Sally

If you like this, try Shostakovich's Symphony No. 10

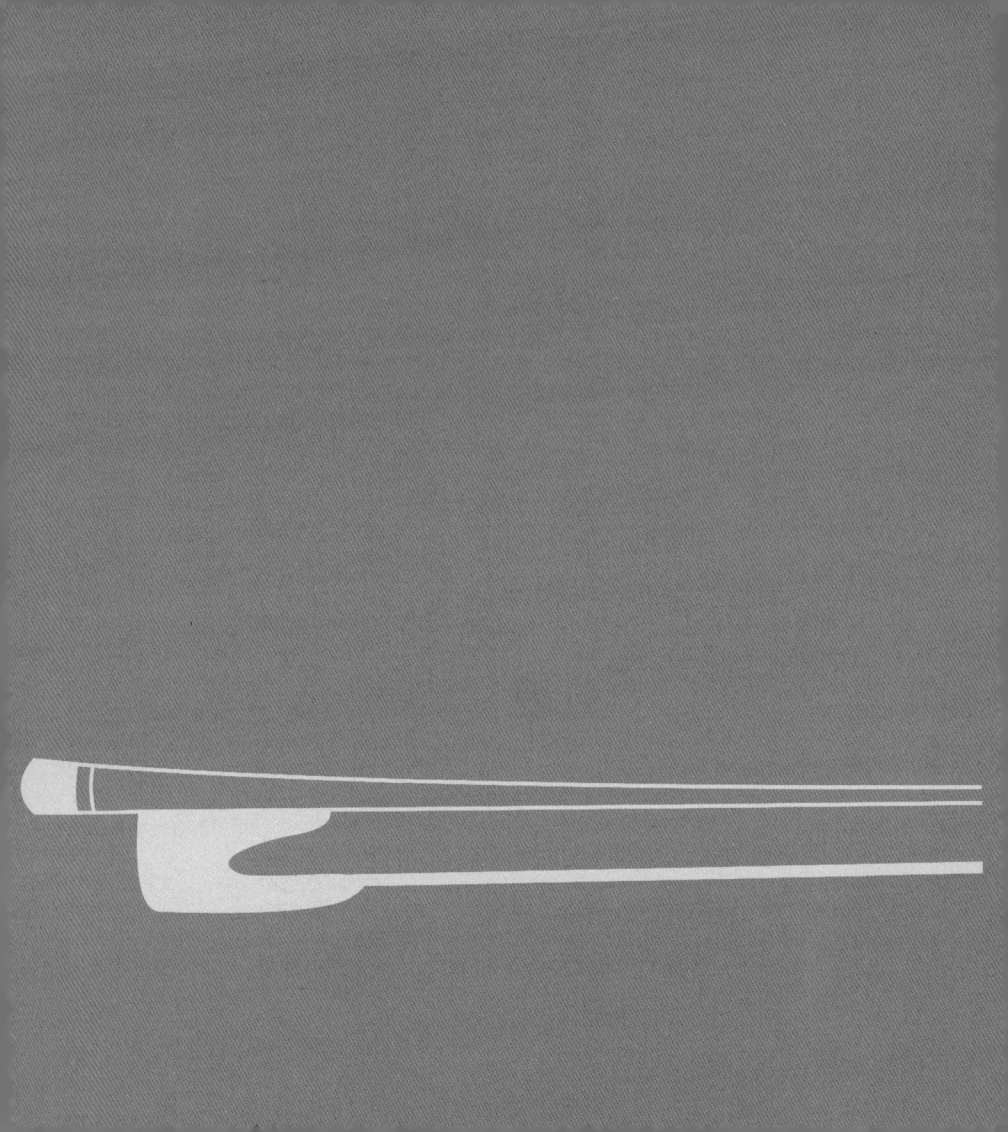

COLLECTION THREE

IF YOU'RE FEELING A LITTLE MORE ADVENTUROUS

"Breathtaking"

TALLIS – SPEM IN ALIUM (c.1570)
Jeremy Summerly, Oxford Camerata
Naxos 8557770 Released 23 May 2005

Quite simply this is Blackwell Music Shop's biggest selling disc in recent years. Released to celebrate the 500th anniversary of Tallis' birth, it features the composer's greatest masterpiece, *Spem in Alium*. This majestic and moving work, written in the composer's maturity, is scored for forty voices and remains unsurpassed in sheer scale and ambition. The performances here come courtesy of Jeremy Summerly and the Oxford Camerata who have brought us previously acclaimed recordings of early music masters such as Dufay, Josquin and Byrd. The interpretation is magnificent - as inspired as the work itself. Presented here alongside several other sublime Tallis works, this CD represents truly astonishing value. Ben

If you like this, try Gesualdo's Madrigals

BACH, J. S. – ORGAN WORKS (c.1700 –1715)
Wolfgang Rubsam and Bertalen Hock
Naxos 8553859 Released 4 November 1996

There exists a bewilderingly large array of Bach organ works on disc and it's hard for the non-expert to decide where to start in building a collection. This disc provides a good way in, beginning as it does with one of the best known works for organ, the *Toccata and Fugue* BWV565, performed here characterfully and with great flair by Wolfgang Rubsam on the warm-toned Flentrop organ at Oberlin College, Ohio. His reading of the weighty E♭ major *Prelude and Fugue* BWV552 is magnificent and stately, the *Chorale Prelude* BWV639 and the Adagio from BWV564 highly lyrical. Bertalan Hock, the other organist on this disc, provides the pre-wedding favourite *Jesu, joy of man's desiring* to complete the set. Tom

If you like this, try J. S. Bach's *Well-Tempered Clavier*

VARIOUS – BAROQUE SUITES AND CONCERTOS
(1722–1749)
Various Artists
Decca 4674152 Released 5 February 2001

This disc boasts the fine playing of the Academy of St Martin-in-the-Fields (under the baton of Sir Neville Marriner) who give a spirited rendering of Handel's *Royal Fireworks* music and Telemann's grand *Overture in D major* and Viola Concerto. The Stuttgart Chamber Orchestra and Karl Munchinger meanwhile leave us with stylish versions of the ever-popular *Adagio* by Albinoni, the second and third Orchestral Suites by J. S. Bach and Pergolesi's beautiful but underperformed Flute Concerto No. 2. *Winter* from Vivaldi's *Four Seasons* also features, Konstanty Kulka doing the honours on solo violin. Tom

If you like this, try Pachelbel's *Canon*

MOZART – SERENADE No. 13 EINE KLEINE NACHTMUSIK (1787)
Karl Bohm, Vienna Philharmonic Orchestra
DG 4394722 Released 10 January 1995

This budget-price disc contains three of Mozart's later works, written before his untimely death at the age of 35. *Eine kleine Nachtmusik*, or *A Little Night Music*, stands as one of the composer's most famous and most popular works. Written in 1787, this serenade could have served as light relief from the opera Mozart was writing at the same time, *Don Giovanni*. However, as Bohm displays in this recording, the simple lyricism and lightness of feeling on the surface conceal the more shadowy, troubled depths of night-time. Also featuring symphonies forty and forty-one, this is a fine survey of a rich period in the composer's life. Ben

If you like this, try Mozart's *Musical Joke*

HAYDN – STRING QUARTETS OPUS 64, Nos. 4–6 (1790)
Kodály Quartet
Naxos 8550674 Released 1 August 1993

Among the most popular of the many string quartets Haydn wrote, the six Opus 64 quartets are full of grace and charm. The most instantly likeable of these is certainly No. 5, the *Lark*, named after the glorious soaring melody that opens the first movement. The Kodály Quartet give characteristically refined, mature interpretations of these pieces - their style is reserved and studious, but full of character. This balance is particularly well illustrated by their masterful handling of the *Lark's* frantic last movement, and by a languid rendition of the slow movement of No. 6. Sally

If you like this, try Haydn's Opus 74 String Quartets

MOZART – REQUIEM (1791)
Richard Hickox, Northern Sinfonia
Virgin Classics 5624782 Released 2 August 2004

Buy this disc for the superb choral singing of the London Sinfonia Chorus. They are on fine form under Richard Hickox and relish the chance to show off their large expressive pallet; just listen to the contrast between the thrilling attack of the tenors and basses at the start of the 'Confutatis' and the smooth lyricism of the sopranos and altos moments later. The solo quartet is lead by a powerful Yvonne Kennedy who sings with great charm, if perhaps with a little too much weight in some of the lighter sections. This disc really is twice as good and half as expensive as the competition. Tom

If you like this, try Mozart's *Coronation Mass*

BEETHOVEN – PIANO CONCERTOS Nos. 2 AND 5 EMPEROR (1793 REVISED 1794-1795 AND 1809)
Artur Rubinstein, Daniel Barenboim, London Philharmonic Orchestra
RCA 82876658382 Released 14 March 2005

Originally recorded in 1975 as part of Rubinstein's third round of the Beethoven concertos, this set combines the maturity and vast experience of the legendary pianist with the youthful, vibrant conducting of the young Daniel Barenboim, and the results are wonderful. Though 87 at the time of recording, Rubinstein's fingers had lost none of their speed and nimbleness, and his mastery at the keyboard shines. Of particular note is the Finale of the fifth concerto - Barenboim and Rubinstein weave together the varying textures and moods of the movement with consummate skill and perfect balance, well captured by the sound engineers. In all, a fine offering. Luke W

If you like this, try Beethoven's Violin Concerto

SCHUBERT – LIEDER (1815–1826)
Simon Keenlyside, Malcolm Martineau
Classics for Pleasure 5856182 Released 1 September 2003

This is a real gem of a collection from an artist who is comparatively elusive on disc despite his flourishing recital and stage career. It is Keenlyside's finely-honed dramatic instinct which really distinguishes this recording, particularly in the intense declamatory monologues such as *Gruppe aus dem Tartarus*, though his mellifluous, firm-textured baritone is equally convincing in the more lyrical songs. The selection of Lieder is also exemplary, including favourites such as *Heidenröslein* and *Du bist die Ruh* (which Keenlyside imbues with freshness and a textual sensitivity that never lapses into mannerism) as well as several comparative rarities. A glorious recital from a charismatic singer in his prime. Kath

If you like this, try Schubert's *Winterreise*

ROSSINI – THE BARBER OF SEVILLE HIGHLIGHTS (1816)
Sonia Ganassi, Roberto Servile, Ramon Vargas, Will Humburg,
Budapest Failoni Chamber Orchestra
Naxos 8553436 Released 1 November 1997

This disc of highlights from Naxos' excellent 3-disc set (866002729) provides a generous 79 minutes of superb music making. The cast is lead by star-in-the-making Ramon Vargas as Almaviva. He copes with the often high tessitura of the part admirably and sails through the many florid passages with ease. The rest of the cast sing with great freshness and manage to capture the sense of fun that should pervade any successful performance of this comedy. The almost-aptly-named Figaro, sung by Roberto Servile, and Rosina, performed by Sonia Ganassi, give particularly characterful performances in their respective arias, and especially in the duet 'Dunque io son'. Tom

If you like this, try Donizetti's *Don Pasquale*

BEETHOVEN – SYMPHONY No. 9 CHORAL (1822–1824)
Wilhelm Fürtwangler, Bayreuth Festival Chorus & Orchestra
EMI Classics 5669012 Released 1 November 1998

Beethoven's *Choral* Symphony is well served on disc. What makes Fürtwangler's account stand out is its depth of emotion and power of expression. Recorded live at the first opening of the Bayreuth Festspielhaus since the Second World War the listener is at once aware of the moving atmosphere of this historic occasion; it is no coincidence that the 'Ode to Joy' from the final movement has since come to symbolise European Unity. The playing is of the first order and the singing, especially of the solo quartet, is as good as one could hope to find. Tom

If you like this, try Beethoven's Symphony No. 7

MENDELSSOHN – OVERTURES (1824–1839)
Claudio Abbado, London Symphony Orchestra
DG 4231042 Released 1 February 1988

From the *Hebrides*, a vivid orchestral depiction of a sea voyage, to the light and playful *A Midsummer Night's Dream*, Mendelssohn's overtures sparkle with character and charm. All of his most well-loved overtures are included on this superlative recording, with the LSO giving energetic and exuberant performances under Claudio Abbado. A particular highlight of the disc is the inclusion of a truly expressive rendering of *The Tale of the Fair Melusine*, a gem of a piece that is all too often overlooked. Sally

If you like this, try Mendelssohn's Symphony No. 3 *Scottish*

SCHUMANN – SYMPHONY No. 1 SPRING (1841)
John Eliot Gardiner, Orchestre Revolutionnaire et Romantique
Archiv Produktion 4745512 Released 20 October 2003

Gardiner leads the Orchestre Revolutionnaire et Romantique in a youthful performance of Schumann's *Spring* Symphony. Playing on period instruments the timbre is mellow and sweet. The brooding introduction gives way to a sparkling Allegro, matched in its breathtaking speed by the frantic Scherzo. Whilst listening to this recording in the shop, a customer not previously well-acquainted with Schumann bought a copy there and then; a strong testament to its immediate appeal. The rest of the two-disc set comprises two versions of Symphony No. 4, an early, incomplete, *Symphony in G minor* and the really rather wonderful *Konzertstück* for four horns and orchestra. Tom

If you like this, try Schumann's Symphony No. 3 *Rhenish*

LISZT – PIANO CONCERTOS Nos. 1 AND 2
(1849 REVISED 1853/1856 AND 1839 REVISED 1849–1861)
John Ogdon, Constantin Silvestri, Bournemouth Symphony
Orchestra & Colin Davis
BBC Legends BBCL40892 Released 7 January 2002

Ogdon, one of the finest British pianists of the last century, will always be remembered for his spell-binding virtuosity which allowed him to conquer feared repertoire - including Busoni's Concerto and Sorabji's gargantuan *Opus Clavicembalisticum*. Ogdon's legendary virtuosity is on show here; the fearsome octaves that open the first concerto are awe-inspiring in his hands, and he is equally impressive when playing a delicate 'pianissimo' at the top register of the piano. Throughout the CD, empty bravura or showmanship never take hold of Liszt's music (Ogdon's deep musicality was an ever-present component of his technique). Solo works, including the first *Mephisto Waltz*, are generous bonuses on this wonderful disc. Luke W

If you like this, try Liszt's *Hungarian Rhapsodies*

SMETANA – MA VLAST (1872–1879)
Antoni Wit, Polish National Radio Symphony Orchestra
Naxos 8550931 Released 15 December 1994

Ma Vlast (*My Country*), Smetana's sweeping set of symphonic poems, describe in evocative musical language the many and varied landscapes of the Bohemian region of eastern Europe, interspersed with programmatic pieces describing the careers of some of the area's greatest mythical and historical figures. With the exception of 'Vltava', this is not a well-known work, and judging by the performances presented on this disc, this is a great shame. The orchestral performance is tight and well-controlled by Wit, and the performances capture the spaciousness and drama of this exciting set very well indeed. Luke W

If you like this, try Smetana's opera *The Bartered Bride*

BRUCKNER – SYMPHONY No. 4
(1874 REVISED 1878-1880 AND 1886)
Georg Tintner, Royal Scottish National Orchestra
Naxos 8554128 Released 1 January 1999

The symphonies of Anton Bruckner have often been described as "cathedrals of sound" in reference to their great spaciousness and grandeur. Bruckner was rather insecure with regard to his musical output, constantly revising his work and even nullifying a symphony he had written prior to discovering his hero Wagner. His revisions were often misguided, but in the case of his fourth symphony (the *"Romantic"*) he made great improvements, in particular with the replacement of an unremarkable third movement with the thrilling 'Hunting' scherzo. The powerful drama of this symphony is well represented here in a lyrical performance by Tintner and the Royal Scottish National Orchestra. Sally

If you like this, try Bruckner's Symphony No. 7

TCHAIKOVSKY – PIANO CONCERTO NO. 1 (1878)
John Browning, Seiji Ozawa, London Symphony Orchestra
RCA 09026639792 Released 3 February 2003

When presented with the newly-written score for Tchaikovsky's first piano concerto, the great pianist Nikolay Rubinstein rejected the piece, claiming that it was unplayable and worthless. But Rubinstein was soon forced to eat his words; the first performance was a resounding success, and the concerto has remained a firm favourite with concert-goers ever since. John Browning's passionate and powerful performance is here paired with a studious interpretation of Tchaikovsky's Violin Concerto performed by Erick Friedman, whose gorgeous, lyrical violin playing is a true joy to listen to. Sally

If you like this, try Tchaikovsky's *Variations on a Rococo Theme*

BRAHMS – PIANO CONCERTO No. 2 (1878–1881)
Claudio Arrau, Bernard Haitink, Amsterdam Concertgebouw Orchestra
Philips 4383202 Released 1 June 1993

Brahms was one of the last great Romantic composers, and while remaining true to traditional musical form, his work is adventurous in harmony and texture. His piano concertos are perfect tests of a pianist's skill and virtuosity - the first is full of opportunities for showing off, while the second is one of the most difficult pieces in the repertoire. Arrau's accounts of these works are fresh and sparkling, in a set that also includes two nicely contrasting pieces: the humorous *Academic Festival Overture* and the tormented *Tragic Overture* - in the (translated) words of Brahms himself, "one laughs while the other cries". Sally

If you like this, try Brahms's *Rhapsodies and Intermezzi*

TCHAIKOVSKY – 1812 OVERTURE (1880)
Adrian Leaper, Royal Philharmonic Orchestra
Naxos 8550500 Released 31 December 1993

Adrian Leaper and the Royal Philharmonic Orchestra show their mettle in this exciting and engaging account of Tchaikovsky's fiery overture. Many performances overstress the bombastic qualities of the work at the expense of the more intimate moments. Leaper is not guilty of this and allows the many charming melodies in the score a natural flow. Where more force is required the brass produce a fine, weighty sound and the cannon makes a full impact when its moment arrives. The *1812* is joined on this disc by the *Capriccio Italien*, *Marche Slave* and *Romeo and Juliet Overture*. Tom

If you like this, try Tchaikovsky's tone poem *Francesca da Rimini*

SULLIVAN (AND GILBERT) – YEOMEN OF THE GUARD (1888)
Malcolm Sargent, D'Oyly Carte Opera Chours
Decca 4736652 Released 24 March 2003

The closest that Gilbert and Sullivan came to writing 'serious' opera, *The Yeomen of the Guard* takes as its subject the gory Tower of London, mingling the classic Savoy frivolity with several moments of true sentiment. From the exuberant opening of the overture to the tragic chords that end the finale, Sir Malcolm Sargent's conducting is full of energy, while achieving appropriate restraint for the more subdued sections (such as the wistful 'Strange Adventure'). John Reed is on his best form as the jester Jack Point, while Philip Potter makes a clear-toned Fairfax. The opera is here paired with a light-hearted rendition of *Trial By Jury*. Sally

If you like this, try Offenbach's opera *Orpheus in the Underworld*

STRAUSS, R. – ALSO SPRACH ZARATHUSTRA (1895–1896)
Herbert von Karajan, Berlin Philharmonic Orchestra
DG 4474412 Released 18 September 1995

The combination of Karajan and the Berlin Philharmonic is a particularly fine one, and never more so than in the repertoire of the great German romantics such as Richard Strauss. Karajan's *Also sprach Zarathustra* is one of the best on record: Karajan squeezes every drop of emotion from his players, without once becoming affected or melodramatic. He also exploits the full range of the BPO's tonal palette, from the vastly spacious opening to the impassioned *Joys and Passions* to the delicacy of *The Backworldsmen*. Also included are the tone poems *Till Eugenspiel* and *Don Juan*, as well as the 'Tanze der sieben Schleien' from *Salome*. Luke W

If you like this, try Richard Strauss' opera *Der Rosenkavalier*

ELGAR – VARIATIONS ON AN ORIGINAL THEME ENIGMA (1898–1899)
Bryden Thomson, London Philharmonic Orchestra
Chandos CHAN6692 Released 14 June 2004

One of Elgar's best-loved masterpieces, the *Enigma* Variations appears, on this occasion, alongside some lesser-known works. The boomy acoustic of All Saints in Tooting lessers the crisp, dry attack so essential to such variations as 'Troyte' or 'G.R.S.', though conversly, the expansive reverb provides a sublime warm bed for the mellifluous contours of 'R.P.A.', 'W.N.' and 'Nimord', for example. Always an area of fascination concerning this work, the disc stands as one of the few rare recordings of *Enigma* that remains faithful to Elgar's tempi throughout. Indeed, Thomson's main concern it seems is to almost simply 'update' the historic EMI recording of 1932 with the LSO conducted by Elgar himself, in an utterly refined and beautifully crafted manner. Hugh

If you like this, try Elgar's Cello Concerto

SIBELIUS – FINLANDIA (1899 REVISED 1900)
Petri Sakari, Iceland Symphony Orchestra
Naxos 8554265 Released 1 October 1999

Sibelius is quoted as having said, "Give me the loneliness either of the Finnish forest or of a big city", and such temperaments are clearly apparent in his powerful and earthy music. This recording offsets the jubilance and festivity of the *Karelia Suite* with the more subdued tones of *The Swan of Tuonela*, whose sublime poetry crowns the *Lemminkainen Suite*. For many, the highlight of the disc will be the Iceland Symphony Orchestra's passionate account of *Finlandia*, which is perhaps Sibelius' best-known work. Sally

If you like this, try Sibelius' Symphony No. 2

PUCCINI – OPERA HIGHLIGHTS (1893–1926)
Maria Callas
Regis RRC1234 Released 2 January 2006

Recorded when the iconic Greek soprano Maria Callas was in her prime, this all-Puccini disc is a wonderful introduction to Italian verismo opera: as well as arias from *Il Trittico, La Bohème, Manon Lescaut,* and *Turandot,* the disc includes substantial highlights from Karajan's acclaimed 1954 recording of *Madama Butterfly.* Though Callas sang an astounding range of roles throughout her career, her lustrous dark-hued soprano is ideally suited to Puccini's soaring lines and dramatic climaxes. Her versatility is in evidence even within this single-composer recital, with each of Puccini's heroines subtly delineated: Callas is mesmerising as both the sadistic princess Turandot and the vulnerable slave-girl Liu. Kath

If you like this, try Puccini's *Tosca*

SCHOENBERG – FIVE ORCHESTRAL PIECES (1909)
Simone Rattle, CBSO
EMI Classics 5758802 Released 3 February 2003

Known as the Second Viennese School, the trio of Schoenberg, Webern and Berg were responsible for the compositional technique of serialism. A logical development of the expressive harmony of the late Romantics, these pieces show serialism in a variety of guises. Schoenberg's *Five Orchestral Pieces* pre-date his serial language and retain a sense of Romantic expression and form; Webern's Variations explore the potentials of tonal microcosms and miniature structures; finally, Berg's *Lulu Suite* demonstrates the capacity of serialism to express emotions such as despair and hysteria. Magnificently played by the CBSO under a young Simon Rattle, this set is a fine introduction to twentieth-century modernism. Luke W

If you like this, try Schoenberg's *Gurrelieder*

VAUGHAN WILLIAMS – THE LARK ASCENDING
(1914 REVISED 1920)
Sarah Chang, Bernard Haitink, London Philharmonic Orchestra
EMI Classics 5851512 Released 13 October 2003

Ralph Vaughan Williams remains one of the most characteristically "English" composers, and this offering gives an excellent overview of all aspects of his output. *On Wenlock Edge* is one of Vaughan Williams' finest song cycles, and Ian Bostridge captures the spirit of Housman's poetry perfectly. *In the Fen Country* demonstrates Vaughan Williams' capacity to evoke English landscapes, while his love of folksong (and of the underrated viola) is expressed in *Norfolk Rhapsody No. 1*. Sarah Chang soars above beautifully balanced strings in *The Lark Ascending*, and the quality of string sound shines through in the *Fantasia on a theme by Thomas Tallis*, one of Vaughan Williams' best-loved and most widely-played works. Luke W

If you like this, try Vaughan Williams' *Dives and Lazarus*

WALTON – SYMPHONY NO. 1 (1931-1935)
André Previn, London Symphony Orchestra
RCA 74321925752 Released 4 March 2002

This recording of Walton's first symphony did much to ensure a place in the canon for a work which had not initially received the recognition that it deserved. What really distinguishes Previn's account is his remarkable ability to balance the jazz and Romantic elements of this bizarre but powerful work, revelling in Walton's punchy syncopation and brash brass writing but also coaxing some gorgeously lyrical playing from the strings and woodwind. The conductor's background in jazz and film music is evident throughout. Previn maintains total control over both the manic, irregular rhythms of Walton's score, and his own breakneck tempo. This two-CD set also features the first-ever recording of Walton's Cello Concerto, and boasts a surprising clarity of sound for recordings made in the 1960s. Kath

If you like this, try Walton's *Belshazzar's Feast*

ORFF – CARMINA BURANA (1936)
Eugene Ormandy, Rutgers University Choir, Philadelphia Orchestra
Sony Classical SBK47668 Released 19 November 2001

From the very first bar of *Carmina Burana*, the listener is transported into a world of dionysian delight and medieval mischief. This is one of the most well-loved and renowned pieces of classical music, instantly recognisable from countless appearances on film and television, not to mention its accompaniment to a commerical for a certain men's aftershave. With set-pieces titled *In Spring*, *In the Tavern* and *The Court of Love*, the work oozes sensuality and excitement. On this CD, Ormandy brings the theatricality and sheer joy of the work to the fore, with soloists, chorus and orchestra combining to create an exhilarating musical feast. Ben

If you like this, try Mahler's cantata *Das Klagende Lied*

PROKOFIEV – ROMEO AND JULIET HIGHLIGHTS (1938)
Mariss Jansons, Oslo Philharmonic Orchestra
EMI 5752272 Released 3 June 2002

Music for the stage constitutes a large percentage of Prokofiev's output, but he frequently found himself frustrated by the complications imposed upon the music by considerations of staging. As a case in point, it was at one point his intention to change the ending of his ballet *Romeo and Juliet* to a happy one - after all, dead people can't dance! To free the music from the fetters of theatre, he often extracted suites from his operas and ballets. On this disc, Jansons conducts an energetic performance of the concert suites of *Romeo and Juliet*, with a particularly vigorous rendition of the famous 'Montagues and Capulets' theme. Sally

If you like this, try Prokofiev's *Classical Symphony*

MESSIAEN – TURANGALILA SYMPHONIE (1946–1948)
Simon Rattle, CBSO
EMI Classics 5865252 Released 4 April 2005

Olivier Messiaen's *Turangalila Symphonie* stands as one of the major musical works of the twentieth century. The work is of epic proportions as the composer attempts to convey his profound love of humanity, of God, and of the natural world around him. From the very beginning we are transported into a unique sound world. The score calls for huge resources including enlarged brass and percussion sections, a ferociously difficult piano part and, most famously, the electronic whirls of the ondes martenot. Simon Rattle truly understands this music, with its traces of modernist, Eastern, and jazz styles. There is an electrifying beauty to this recording and as the final chord dies away we are left in awe of this wonderful work. Ben

If you like this, try Messiaen's *Catalogue d'oiseaux*

ADAMS – SHAKER LOOPS (1983)
Christopher Warren-Green, London Chamber Orchestra
Virgin Classics 3633082 Released 7 August 2006

This bargain-price CD provides an ideal introduction to one of the most influential musical styles of our time - Minimalism. The likes of John Adams, Philip Glass and Steve Reich have inspired a generation of composers in the concert hall, on the big screen, and in more experimental pop music. The rhythmic intensity and drive that this music displays is captured in these wonderfully inspired performances. At this price, you are guaranteed a treat. Ben

If you like this, try Gershwin's *An American in Paris*

INDEX

INDEX ALPHABETICAL BY COMPOSER

Adams – Shaker Loops (1983)	44
Bach, J. S. – Brandenburg Concertos (1708–1721)	12
Bach, J. S. – St John Passion (1724 revised c.1730 and again late 1740s)	18
Bach, J. S. – Organ Works (c.1700–1715)	30
Beethoven – Piano Concertos Nos. 2 and 5 Emperor (1793 revised 1794–1795 and 1809)	33
Beethoven – Sonata for Piano No. 14 Moonlight (1801)	13
Beethoven – Symphonies Nos. 5 and 6 (1807 and 1808)	20
Beethoven – Symphony No. 9 Choral (1822-1824)	34
Berlioz – Symphonie Fantastique (1830)	21
Bizet – Carmen Highlights (1875)	15
Brahms – Piano Concerto No. 2 (1878–1881)	38
Bruckner – Symphony No. 4 (1874 revised 1878–1880 and 1886)	37
Chopin – Piano Works (1829–1846)	22
Debussy – La Mer (1903–1905)	26
Dvořák – Symphony No. 9 From The New World (1893)	25
Elgar – Variations on an Original Theme Enigma (1898–1899)	40
Gershwin – Rhapsody in Blue (1924)	16
Grieg – Piano Concerto (1868)	14
Handel – Messiah (1742 revised 1751)	12
Handel – Music for Royal Fireworks and Water Music (1749 and 1715–1717 revised 1736)	19
Haydn – String Quartets Opus 64 (1790)	32
Haydn – Symphonies Nos. 99–104 (1793–1795)	20
Holst – The Planets (1916)	27
Liszt – Piano Concertos Nos. 1 and 2 (1849 revised 1853/1856 and 1839 revised 1849–1861)	36
Mahler – Symphony No. 5 (1901–1902)	25
Mendelssohn – Overtures (1824–1839)	35
Mendelssohn – Violin Concerto (1844)	22
Messiaen – Turangalila Symphonie (1946–1948)	44
Mozart – Serenade No. 13 Eine Kleine Nachtmusik (1787)	31

Mozart – Clarinet Concerto (1791)	13
Mozart – Magic Flute Highlights (1791)	19
Mozart – Requiem (1791)	32
Mussorgsky – A Night on the Bare Mountain (1867 re-orchestrated 1886)	23
Orff – Carmina Burana (1936)	43
Prokofiev – Romeo and Juliet Highlights (1938)	43
Puccini – Opera Highlights (1893–1926)	41
Rachmaninov – Piano Concerto No. 2 (1900–1901)	16
Rossini – The Barber of Seville Highlights (1816)	34
Saint-Saëns – Carnaval des Animaux (Carnival of the Animals) (1886)	24
Schoenberg – Five Orchestral Pieces (1909)	41
Schubert – Lieder (1815–1826)	33
Schubert – Symphonies Nos. 5, 8 and 9 (1816, 1822 and 1825–1828)	21
Schumann – Symphony No. 1 Spring (1841)	35
Shostakovich – Symphony No. 5 (1937)	27
Sibelius – Finlandia (1899 revised 1900)	40
Smetana – Ma Vlast (1872–1879)	36
Strauss R – Also sprach Zarathustra (1895-1896)	39
Stravinsky – The Firebird (1910)	26
Sullivan (and Gilbert) – Yeomen of the Guard (1888)	39
Tallis – Spem in Alium (c.1570)	30
Tchaikovsky – Piano Concerto No. 1 (1875)	37
Tchaikovsky – Swan Lake Highlights (1876)	24
Tchaikovsky – Symphonies Nos. 4–6 (1877, 1888 and 1893)	15
Tchaikovsky – 1812 Overture (1880)	38
Various – Baroque Suites and Concertos (1722–1749)	31
Vaughan Williams – The Lark Ascending (1914 revised 1920)	42
Verdi – Aida (1871)	23
Vivaldi – Concerti for Violin and Strings Four Seasons (1725)	18
Wagner – Overtures (1841–1874)	14
Walton – Symphony No. 1 (1931–1935)	42

INDEX CHRONOLOGICAL BY DATE OF COMPOSITION

Tallis – Spem in Alium (c.1570)	30
Bach, J. S. – Organ Works (c.1700–1715)	30
Bach, J. S. – Brandenburg Concertos (1708–1721)	12
Various – Baroque Suites and Concertos (1722–1749)	31
Bach J. S. – St John Passion (1724 revised c.1730 and again late 1740s)	18
Vivaldi – Concerti for Violin and Strings Four Seasons (1725)	18
Handel – Messiah (1742 revised 1751)	12
Handel – Music for Royal Fireworks and Water Music (1749 and 1715–1717 revised 1736)	19
Mozart – Serenade No. 13 Eine Kleine Nachtmusik (1787)	31
Haydn – String Quartets Opus 64 (1790)	32
Mozart – Clarinet Concerto (1791)	13
Mozart – Magic Flute Highlights (1791)	19
Mozart – Requiem (1791)	32
Haydn – Symphonies Nos. 99–104 (1793–1795)	20
Beethoven – Piano Concertos Nos. 2 and 5 Emperor (1793 revised 1794–1795 and 1809)	33
Beethoven – Sonata for Piano No. 14 Moonlight (1801)	13
Beethoven – Symphonies Nos. 5 and 6 (1807 and 1808)	20
Schubert – Lieder (1815–1826)	33
Schubert – Symphonies Nos. 5, 8 and 9 (1816, 1822 and 1825–1828)	21
Rossini – The Barber of Seville Highlights (1816)	34
Beethoven – Symphony No. 9 Choral (1822–1824)	34
Mendelssohn – Overtures (1824–1839)	35
Chopin – Piano Works (1829–1846)	22
Berlioz – Symphonie Fantastique (1830)	21
Schumann – Symphony No. 1 Spring (1841)	35
Wagner – Overtures (1841–1874)	14
Mendelssohn – Violin Concerto (1844)	22
Liszt – Piano Concertos Nos. 1 and 2 (1849 revised 1853/1856 and 1839 revised 1849–1861)	36
Mussorgsky – A Night on the Bare Mountain (1867 re-orchestrated 1886)	23

Grieg – Piano Concerto (1868)	14
Verdi – Aida (1871)	23
Smetana – Ma Vlast (1872–1879)	36
Bruckner – Symphony No. 4 (1874 revised 1878–1880 and 1886)	37
Bizet – Carmen Highlights (1875)	15
Tchaikovsky – Piano Concerto No. 1 (1875)	37
Tchaikovsky – Swan Lake Highlights (1876)	24
Tchaikovsky – Symphonies Nos. 4–6 (1877, 1888 and 1893)	15
Brahms – Piano Concerto No. 2 (1878–1881)	38
Tchaikovsky – 1812 Overture (1880)	38
Saint-Saëns – Carnaval des Animaux (Carnival of the Animals) (1886)	24
Sullivan (and Gilbert) – Yeomen of the Guard (1888)	39
Dvořák – Symphony No. 9 From the New World (1893)	25
Puccini – Opera Highlights (1893–1926)	41
Strauss R – Also sprach Zarathustra (1895–1896)	39
Elgar – Variations on an Original Theme Enigma (1898–1899)	40
Sibelius – Finlandia (1899 revised 1900)	40
Rachmaninov – Piano Concerto No. 2 (1900–1901)	16
Mahler – Symphony No. 5 (1901–1902)	25
Debussy – La Mer (1903–1905)	26
Schoenberg – Five Orchestral Pieces (1909)	41
Stravinsky – The Firebird (1910)	26
Vaughan Williams – The Lark Ascending (1914 revised 1920)	42
Holst – The Planets (1916)	27
Gershwin – Rhapsody in Blue (1924)	16
Walton – Symphony No. 1 (1931–1935)	42
Orff – Carmina Burana (1936)	43
Shostakovich – Symphony No. 5 (1937)	27
Prokofiev – Romeo and Juliet Highlights (1938)	43
Messiaen – Turangalila Symphonie (1946–1948)	44
Adams – Shaker Loops (1983)	44

THE AUTHORS

Katherine Cooper (Recordings Specialist)
Katherine read English at University College, Oxford, and did postgraduate work at York and Kingston, where she is now in the final stages of a doctorate on twentieth-century pastoralism. She is an active viola player and mezzo, with recent opera roles including Dorabella, Cherubino, Donna Elvira, and Mrs Grose in Britten's *The Turn of the Screw*.

Sally Outen
Sally joined Blackwell shortly after completing her Biology degree at Oxford in 2005. As a singer, she has enjoyed a number of roles in light opera with the university's Gilbert and Sullivan Society, as well as performing with various chapel choirs. She plays the piano, organ and double bass.

Luke Wilcox
Luke read Music at Magdalen College, Oxford, where he played in both the Oxford University Orchestra and Oxford University Philharmonia. He also works in the fields of complementary health and Chinese medicine, and maintains an active research interest in ancient Chinese music theory and history.

Ben Hall
Prior to working at Blackwell, Ben's career highlight was as an advisory member to the Young Offenders' Theatre Group, 'Break Out'. Productions included 'My Heart Skipped a Beat', a romantic musical comedy set in a hospital ward. Ben continues to take an academic interest in the relationship between music and society, both as composer and advisor.

Tom West
Tom read Law at Corpus Christi, Oxford, where he was an organ scholar, and at the Oxford Institute of Legal Practice. Now also Director of Music at All Saints Church in Headington, he is much in demand as an accompanist and organ soloist and has sung principal roles in *Don Giovanni, La Bohème* and *Cosi Fan Tutte* as well as being an active member of the University Gilbert & Sullivan Society.

Rachel Parris
Rachel studied Music at St Hilda's College, Oxford. A first-study pianist, she has given recitals at the Jacqueline Du Pré building and the Holywell Music Room, and has conducted for various college choirs and theatre productions. She also enjoys diverse vocal interests, dividing much of her time between singing Renaissance madrigals in an early music ensemble and performing bawdy cabaret with a travelling burlesque troupe.

Luke Berryman
Luke is an undergraduate reading Music at Magdalen College, Oxford. He studies piano with Niel Immelman, and has given regular concerts in Oxfordshire, in venues including the Holywell Music Room, the Jacqueline Du Pré Building, and the Sheldonian Theatre. One appearance of note was as soloist in Tchaikovsky's second Piano Concerto. He is currently in his final year at Oxford.

Hugh Brunt
Hugh is studying Music at New College, Oxford, on a choral scholarship. He is active both as a composer and conductor. Recent works have received performances at The Sage Gateshead (televised on BBC) and the Wigmore Hall. Hugh is also conductor of the Oxford New Orchestra and Oxford University Philharmonia.

You can purchase these CDs from Blackwell Online
or from our music shops in Oxford and Cambridge.

www.blackwell.co.uk/cd

Blackwell Music, 23-25 Broad Street, Oxford
Tel 01865 333581 E-mail cds.music@blackwell.co.uk

Heffers Sound, 19 Trinity Street, Cambridge
Tel 01223 568562 E-mail sound@heffers.co.uk

The information contained in this publication has been published in good faith
and every effort has been made to ensure its accuracy. Blackwell cannot accept
any responsibility for any error or misinterpretation or changes by third parties.